RHYMECOLOGY

Using Hip-Hop To Heal

The Therapist Guide

Using Hip-Hop To Heal

The Therapist Guide

JEFFREY T. WALKER, M.A.

Walker Works Publishing

Rhymecology: Using Hip-Hop To Heal

The Therapist Guide

Author Jeffrey T. Walker

Published by Walker Works Publishing

www.walkerworks.net

Cover Design by Gilli Moon.

Front Cover Headphones Photo © Svetlanka809 | Dreamstime.com

Back over Shadow Of Hand With Microphone Photo © Kentannenbaum | Dreamstime.com

This book is available at quantity discounts for bulk purchases, for information contact the publisher above.

Printed in the United States of America

10	9	8	7	6	5	4	3	2	1

ISBN-13: 978-1517783778 / ISBN-10: 1517783771 (CreateSpace Paperback version)

What They Say

"Rhymecology is hip-hop as therapy. Hip-hop as healing. It is hip-hop beyond entertainment. It is hip-hop that you can actually grow and develop from."
-KRS-One (Hip-hop Legend/Professor/Author)

"This book describes the challenges of working with teens with behavioral and emotional difficulties. Rhymecology is a bridge to marginalized youth, who often have no voice. How smart Jeff Walker is to help this group find a voice, and use it to promote self-expression, healing, and growth."
-Peter Zucker, Ph. D. (Stars Behavioral Health Group, Owner)

"Author / Artist Jeffrey Walker delivers his insightful reflections about the impact of hip-hop on our youth not just as someone who grew up with a love for hip-hop but also as a respected Spoken-Word Artist himself. Add to the mix that he works on the frontlines as a teen counselor / therapist for troubled youth....Mr. Walker knows exactly where these kids are coming from."
-Bob Bryan (Hip-Hop Filmmaker)

Rhymecology is a master lyricist's recipe—quite practical in many ways—for redirecting our words to the places that help, a service that great popular music has always granted."
-Thomas Harrison , Ph.D. (UCLA Professor)

"Of all the characters I've come across in my 10 year recording career, Jeff Walker is the most wholeheartedly dedicated to raising awareness about the side of Hip Hop & Rap music that mainstream media rarely acknowledges. His writings on the complexity of rap lyrics with regard to content, and syllabic and rhythmic structure are a must for the mc/songwriter in training or any artistic naysayers in need of proselytizing."
-Louis Logic (Emcee, Hip-hop Historian)

"Rhymecology is dynamic force that utilizes a language that speaks to inner city youth. Approaching youngsters with a vernacular and format that they can relate to is a creative and effective way to reach this challenged age group. This collection is innovative tool that can be used by clinical staff and youth alike to explore detrimental patterns of behavior and to inspire "what could be" and not just "what is".
-Jessica Plancich, MA, MFT (Infferfinity, Director)

DEDICATION

This book is dedicated to therapists, social workers, counselors, mental health professionals and youth workers who dedicate their lives to healing those in need. You are appreciated.

ACKNOWLEDGMENTS

A huge thank you to my wonderfully artistic, supportive and driven wife Gilli Moon. If there were more of you, this world would be much more colorful, creative and productive.

So much thanks goes to the Hip-Hop artists who continue to make meaningful music with creatively conscious messages, even though it won't sell as much as the commercial crap media pushes on us. Without you this book would be a lot thinner.

Thank you to everyone at Stars Behavioral Health Group for allowing me to incorporate Rhymecology into counseling sessions and allowing me to spread my message to therapists across the country.

Lastly yet mostly, thank you to my parents for always allowing me to follow my passion. Your guidance and love made me who I am.

CONTENTS

TERMINOLOGY

Hip-Hop: A name for the 4 elements of the late 70's New York City renaissance which includes break dancing, emceeing, (rapping) graffiti, and turntablism.

I imagine Hip-Hop as "The Tree". Branches of on the hip-hop tree include emceeing, street art (graffiti), turntabalism (DJing), breakdancing (bboying), spoken word, fashion, dialect and more.

Turntabalism: The art of playing the turntable as a musical instrument. Not to be confused with DJing, which is more about providing dance music and/or mixing beats. Turntablism is more about manipulating sounds and creating rhythms or even melodies by scratching and techniques using a mixer.

Not all DJs are turntablists, but all turntablists (with a few rare exceptions) are DJs.

Emcee: Derived from the original abbreviation "MC," now used as the generic term for anyone who speaks over a beat, or performs songs that could be termed "hip-hop." An emcee is as an artist who lives and breathes the hip-hop culture. An emcee uses his art form to uplift and enlighten.

Rapper: One who expresses himself through the urban street poetry form called "rap". A rapper can be anyone who rhymes words together. Rappers often make songs with the sole goal of selling records regardless of the effect on culture.

In this guide, when I refer to an "emcee", I am paying the highest respect to that artist. When I refer to "rappers" it is often because the artist portrays all the negative stereotypes the media promote about them.

Client: Youth receiving services or assistance from a More Knowledgeable Other (Therapist, Counselor, Teacher or Qualified adult).

SES: Social Economic Status

*: I provided artist, song and album recommendations throughout the guide. If you only have time to find one of the recommendations provided, use the one with the * next to it..

INTRODUCTION

Welcome to the **Rhymecology®: Using Hip-Hop To Heal- The Therapist's Guide**, and congratulations on being a difference maker. If you have picked this up you are most likely someone who cares about youth, whether in a professional or familial way. Thank you for that. We need more people like you.

I am one of you. I have spent my professional life toiling in high risk Southern California streets working with youth. They are often called "at-risk", "urban", "delinquent" and the like, but first they are children. Much more often than not, they were dealt a bad hand. A bad hand can be a result of unskilled/unloving parents, being on the bottom on the socio-economic status (SES), living in dangerous neighborhoods and much more. They are children born into harsh situations and rarely have the support or guidance to make it through unscathed.

They need more. More help. More love. More people to listen to them. More empathy. More avenues to express, discover and create themselves. My hope is that this guide will act as a bridge for you to connect with the youth who may seem out of reach. Being in hip-hop culture has been a huge advantage for me when working in community mental health in the Los Angeles area. Over the years I have learned so much and through this guide I will share techniques and tools which what worked for me and others I have taught.

This guide contains tools and techniques; it has a plethora of songs and artists which represent the pure and therapeutic side to hip-hop. I also point out artists who represent "the other side" and explain why certain children might be drawn to certain artists. I breakdown how one can use hip-hop in a client session and how to bill for the use of hip-hop in session.

Every generation puts a different batch of celebrities up on a pedestal. From the days of Sinatra to Elvis to the Beatles and so forth, we follow our musicians to shows, on the road and now on Twitter. The current generation idolizes hip-hop acts, for good and for bad. I am a hip-hop scholar/head/purist who grew up idolizing emcees from my generation. Hip-hop has helped me in numerous ways but I also followed hip-hop to my detriment. One of the goals of this guide is to take the power away from the rapper and give it back to the youth. By pointing out some of the contradictions and myths in hip-hop and with giving exercises in which they create their own rhymes, our youth will feel more empowered.

The big disclaimer here is that there is no guarantee. There is no guarantee that using hip-hop or Rhymecology® will cure every client/child with whom you use it. Rhymecology® is not a one stop healing shop. You will have to use your skills and intuition as well. The over goal for the Rhymecology® guide is to create rapport (Rap Rapport as I call it) with your clients. When you care about something that intrinsically motivates youth on a daily basis, you are more likely to have natural conversations with them, which leaves you a step closer to helping them heal.

Rap is something

you *do*...

Hip hop is something

you *live*.

- KRS-One

1: HEALING WITH HIP-HOP

Hip-Hop began in the South Bronx of New York City in the early 1970's, initially as a form of cultural expression for African Americans (Chang, 2005). With no adult assistance, the youth of the region created a culture which would soon be called hip-hop. Hip-hop culture rose from the ashes of the South Bronx desolation and has been therapeutic for adolescence ever since.

The creative and expressive use of music can be a powerful therapeutic intervention with children and adolescents (Davis, K. 2010). In terms of sales, downloads and surveys since the mid 1990's, rap music has been the most popular form of music among youth (Tyson, 2002). In 2000, Don Elligan introduced "Rap Therapy" as a psychotherapeutic intervention for working with at-risk youths, primarily African American males whose identities were highly influenced by rap music (Gonzalez & Hayes, 2009). Elligan (2007) declared that rap music is one of the most significant influences on young African American men and that 97 percent of black youth like rap music. Even though, hip-hop has been generally associated with African-American and Latino urban youth, it has moved well beyond urban communities into "mainstream" America (Turner-Musa, 2008).

Although the music has been criticized by religious groups, politicians and women's groups, those who advocate for it claim that it represents the voice of urban youth. They believe it can be valuable as a catalyst to meaningful discussions with those youth (Morrell & Duncan-Andrade 2002). The undeniable influence hip-hop culture has on American youth can be used in therapy and counseling as a way to motivate clients to attend and participate in sessions. As stated by Elligan (2007), considering these facts, psychotherapists who work with this population should become familiar with constructive ways to use rap music in the interest of treatment.

The Need:

The Centers for Disease Control state that homicide is the second leading cause of death for youth between the ages of 10 and 19. It is dangerous and difficult for children in society today and they need to be understood by those who provide therapy to them. They need to feel like therapists care about more than their "problems", that they are genuinely interested in client's likes, dislikes and hobbies.

Pasagiannis (2007) states that despite the treatment cost of over 1.5 billion dollars, at-risk families are less likely to seek treatment and are more often than not end the treatment prematurely. Service providers and researchers note (Slesnick, 2001) that youth with substance abuse problems are difficult to engage in treatment and, when engaged, often drop out early and that a 1988 study found that 62% of youth between the ages of 12–21 were unwilling to come to treatment. Slesnick (2001) stated that treatment completion rates for youths in therapeutic communities have ranged from 10% to 18% only. How can youth be healed if they won't even show up for the treatment?

While the therapeutic process with troubled youth may seem dire, findings have shown how adolescents at-risk can benefit from a creative approach that teaches social and coping skills and can improve their self-awareness and self-esteem (Coholic, 2011). Not only do I believe that using hip-hop music and culture in therapy sessions should be one of those creative approaches, it has already been proven by numerous empirical studies (Tyson, 2002).

While youth may not listen to parents, teachers or therapists as much as adults wish, one thing is evident: they still listen to music. One study showed that of African-American urban youth ages 16-20, 45% indicated they listen to the radio for 3 or more hours daily, are more likely to watch culturally-targeted music videos, and prefer hip-hop/rap music (Turner-Musa, 2008). Another study concluded that the physical aggressiveness of youth appears to be socially sanctioned because of the way that music, movies and videos depict being violent as an admirable way to live life (Spillane-Grieco, 2000). If this is true then it is important for adults to understand hip-hop music and culture so that they can use it to guide wayward youth.

Adults today are fighting for the attention of children. It is increasingly difficult as music and movies are now just "one click away" and many web-based mechanisms with mp3 enabled devices essentially make music "free" and portable (Travis, 2013). With this in mind, using topics like hip-hop, which intrinsically motivate urban children, is very important. I will present a combination of literature, studies and personal experience which proves that hip-hop is a lifestyle choice for urban youth and that it is one of the few things which motivate them.

Brown (2006) stated that children "who lack pro-social skills associated with stable emotional intelligence tend to be easily influenced by various environmental factors such as peers and media" and that this may leave them vulnerable to ideas of sexual promiscuity, violence and other forms of anti-social behavior that are often portrayed in some popular hip-hop media. While premise of this statement will be defended by some and argued by others, what cannot be argued is that the statistics have shown that hip-hop music and culture have been a mainstay in urban as well as wealthy communities for the better part of twenty years and that the importance of assisting these impressionable delinquents by having techniques to build trust with them has never been higher (Tyson, 2002).

While hip-hop's music and fashion are constantly changing, the hold it maintains on urban youth is firm and because of that there is a pressing need for qualified mental health professionals who treat them to use hip-hop in sessions.

2: THE HIP-HOP GENERATION

Today hip-hop is more than music; it is a *culture and a lifestyle*. In terms of sales, downloads and surveys since the mid 1990's, rap music has been the most popular form of music among youth and there is little debate that rap music's universal appeal has led to its current global prominence. Elligan (2007) stated that rap music one of the most significant influences on young African American men and that 97 percent of black youth listen to rap music. Elligan (2007) also stated that considering these facts, psychotherapists who work with this population should become family with constructive ways to use rap music in the interest of treatment.

While youth may not listen to parents, teachers or therapists as much as adults wish, one thing is evident: *they still listen to music*. One study showed that of African-American urban youth ages 16-20, 45% indicated they listen to the radio for 3 or more hours daily, are more likely to watch culturally-targeted music videos, and prefer hip-hop/rap music (Turner-Musa, 2008). Another study concluded that the physical aggressiveness of youth appears to be socially sanctioned because of the way that music, movies and videos depict being violent as an admirable way to live life (Spillane-Grieco, 2000). If this is true then it is important for adults to understand hip-hop music and culture so that they can use it to guide wayward youth.

As stated by Turner-Mesa (2008) hip-hop music "has been shown to play a significant role in decision-making and behavioral choices" among urban youth. Tyson (2002) stated that innovative treatments that are sensitive to a client's culture are important and that client's culture today is based around hip-hop music. Behavior of youth, as reflected in their clothing styles, language usage, jewelry, and automobile preferences, have been attributed to lyrics and videos from the hip-hop industry (Brown, 2006).

As of 2015, it is almost impossible to find a major university without some sort of hip-hop culture class as a part of their curriculum. University of California offers a class on Tupac Shakur; in Denmark one can obtain a Masters degree in Hip-Hop; at the University of Southern California one of the most popular classes is "Rap, Race and Redemption"; and at Harvard University there is a Hip-Hop archive. Hip-hop is infused in education in many places so why is it not playing a bigger part in therapeutic services?

This is where Rhymecology® comes in.

> Rhymecology® embraces the power of hip-hop lyrics and culture and uses them as a therapeutic tool to help people express, discover and create themselves while causing harm to none.

Rhymecology® says that when the raw passion and energy of hip-hop is harnessed and channeled in a positive light, the results are therapeutic. By applying the exercises and information in this guide, counselors, teachers and parents can build a rapport with their children through an unlikely source: Hip-hop.

*"I WANT IT RIGHT AWAY,
I WANT IT RIGHT HERE*

*I WANT TO WRITE GREAT
WORDS THAT FIGHT FEAR"*

TALIB KWELI

3: VALIDATION THROUGH HIP-HOP

Close your eyes and VISUALIZE/feel this with me:

Sitting in class, information flying past you. Failing tests on the same information. The teacher who gives you that information makes a pass at you. An empty seat where your murdered classmate once sat. Meetings at school about you and why you can't understand the information. Walking out of that school with holes in your shoe as your enter a home with no furniture. Sitting on the floor you wonder, not when but IF you will get your next meal. Noticing a bowl of cereal left out from the morning. You grab a plastic spoon ready to take a bite, only to see a roach crawling on the side of the bowl. You give up and go into your room, sit on a mattress with no sheets. You turn on your music, the bass is pumping loud and you hear a rapper say "Ayo, my life is like Roots it's a true story/too gory for them televised fables on cable/Remember that most the cats we know be hustling/my momma worked all of her life, still struggling/I blame it on the government and say it on the radio..." The rapper is angry. The rapper sounds like you. The rapper is feeling things you are feeling and is able to express it in a cool way. Can you imagine how good that feels?

Now imagine that you are sitting on the same mattress with the headphones on and an adult pulls them off your ears and says "I told you I don't want you listening to that stuff!"

First rule of Rhymecology® is an easy one. Don't be the Ipod Police. Nobody wants their choice of music scrutinized. How did you feel when some "old person" (otherwise known as 'adults') told you that what you liked was "not good music"?

When authoritative adults judge, censor or restrict the one medium that understands our population, their emotions are shut down and restricted causing the relationship between authority and child to become a power struggle.

Rap messages are often off base. Much of commercial rap enforces bad stereotypes. The language offends many. **It doesn't matter.**

Listen with them. Empathize. Experience it. Understand what your client loves about hip hop and you will have a better understanding of your client.

The populations which we serve often go through life feeling vilified. They are weighed down by the labels given to them and end up being marginalized. *Just like rap music.* They relate to pain, hardship and struggle and if those feelings stagnate, they tend to feel violent, frustrated and hopeless. *Just like rap music.* By using hip-hop as a catalyst, we can evoke emotions and transform these destructive feelings and cognitions into more supportive outcomes.

4: RAP RAPPORT

"I'M NOT YOUR EVERYDAY RAPPER ON THE MIC THOUGH
I MIGHT SAY SOMETHING YOUR MOTHER DON'T LIKE SO-
DON'T PLAY IT IF SHE'S AROUND TO SEE
BUT YOU CAN'T PLAY THIS CAUSE ITS RATED PG"
- TOO SHORT

Once you and your client are able to listen to various forms of hip-hop together, the rap rapport has begun. "Rap Rapport" is crucial. You may or may not know that much about hip-hop music. However with the help of this guide, you will, at very least, be able to develop rap rapport with your client by playing/showing them examples of classic hip-hop (which can be therapeutic but shhh don't tell them!)

Before a client can feel comfortable talking about hip-hop with you, YOU have to be comfortable with hip-hop itself. Not everyone grows up with hip-hop and not everyone understands (literally and figuratively) hip-hop. I don't understand quantum phsyics, but I am not going to judge anyone who is intrinsically motivated by it or anyone who looks up to physicists. I don't understand the game of cricket at all but I know there are fans who love it as much as I love basketball. So when I sit with cricket fans (can you tell I spend time in Australia?) I ask questions about who is who and what is what, showing my interest in their interest. That is what Rhymecology does for those who might not be as well versed in the beautifully complicated world of hip-hop music.

> You don't have to "like" hip-hop and this does not mean that you have to *approve* of it, but you must *accept* it as the soundtrack of a generation.

Many of your clients are already listening to hip-hop and are going to continue to do so. The thoughts, feelings and actions of clients are often guarded with caregivers and their truer ways expressed with friends as they listen to rap music. <u>We have to change that!</u> If we do nothing else, we have to be able to LISTEN to hip-hop with your clients. From listening to their music with them, we can learn more about them. We will come to understand what evokes them, what they are grieving and what they aspire to be, do and have.

In the following chapters I present some "Listening Sessions" techniques which will help you understand your client and the music they enjoy.

5: THE "MIRROR" TECHNIQUE

Whether in traditional talk therapy or in alternative techniques, many therapists build rapport with the client by being vulnerable. The Rhymecology® method is to discuss songs which are personal or sentimental to you, as a therapist. In fact, it can be powerful to play songs which were either taboo or even "embarrassing" to like at one point. While you play the music, paint a picture for the client describing how your musical taste was negatively perceived. If you did not have that experience, feel free to draw upon stories of classic artists who were once disdained by certain segments of society. The examples of rock and roll groups that were considered threats to authority

"When I look in the mirror

I don't know who I see

sometimes it's like

I don't know who I be

am I even moving at all?

sometimes I can't tell if my life is improving at all"
   -Masta Ace

are plenty (Elvis Presley, The Beatles, and The Rolling Stones just to name a few). Early hip-hop groups had the same effect (Beastie Boys, Public Enemy, Two Live Crew to name a few…sorry, I can't help the accidental rhymes sometimes).

Once the picture has been painted, listen to a song that was considered "taboo" at the time. Listen to it in detail and if applicable, explain how it made you feel at that point in your life. Put clients in your shoes, in hopes that they can soon put you in their shoes. Let them know that you may not be just like them, but, that you can relate.

If you can't think of songs for the occasion, use the list below to marvel at what was once "filth" and "dangerous" for young people to listen to:

"Let's Spend the Night together"-The Rolling Stones
"(You Gotta) Fight for your Right (to Party)"- Beastie Boys
"Like a Virgin"- Madonna

6: THE "PUMP IT UP" TECHNIQUE

Teenagers love their music loud. However, for the most part they don't want to play it very loud around their parents or therapists. If you have an office, plug in their music and turn the speakers up! If you are having a session in the community (i.e. taking them out in your car), let them bring their favorite music. Wherever you think the "comfortable" listening level is, turn it up on more notch (it still won't be near the level the client likes on their own).

You: I'm kind of bored of my music today. How about you introduce me to some new stuff?

Them: Uhhh. I don't think you will like it.

You: Haha, well I'm sure you wouldn't like mine! Just humor me for today. It doesn't matter what it is…in fact, let me hear your favorite artist, even if it is an artist that you would not play in front of most adults.

Them: (Shrugs) Okay.

Put on the music. Nod your head. Tap your finger. Smile when you hear an interesting line. Little to no comments at first. Just let it play. Pay attention to the lyrics. Pay attention to the lyrical theme. Keep your therapists mind open but your therapist mouth shut, for now. If you are not accustomed to listening to hip-hop, it may take time before your ears can dissect the often intricate lyrics. Do whatever you have to do to focus on the song, the client needs to know that you are trying.

If you are able to grasp the theme of your client's music, you will be able to understand them better and be able to use hip-hop to heal more effectively. In the following chapter we will look at various hip-hop themes and how they may be revealing about your client's mindset.

Today and tomorrow is a reflection
of the past
Life's like a cycle and nothing
ever lasts
And being that we're human, we're
forced to play the game
The more things change, the more
they stay the same

- eMC

BONUS TIP:

If your clients do not have CDs or downloading services, you may have to make a small investment to make hip-hop work for you. I recommend that you ask the client to list his/her favorite songs and then go purchase them. Put them on a disk or create a playlist of the songs. Then you can listen to them whenever you are together with the client.

(If would like to make a playlist filled with positive/self-reflective/therapeutic hip-hop songs, don't worry! I've got you covered! Just wait until the end of guide!)

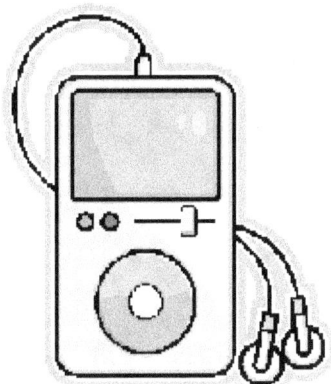

"RAPPERS ARE ALWAYS SAYING THE SAME THING

ABOUT WHAT THE PAIN BRINGS

IN THE FIRST VERSE THEY HAVE AN ICED OUT NECKLACE CHAIN AND RINGS

IN THE NEXT ONE THEIR COMPLAINING THAT THEY GOT NO FAME OR CREAM

SOUND LIKE A BUNCH OF UNDERDEVELOPED PLAYERS ON A LAME TEAM

BUT WHAT MAKES MY BRAIN STING IS

THAT HALF THIS NATIONS CHASING THE SAME THING".

-J.WALKER

7: PRINT IT UP

One important technique to use with youth is reading. Remember when kids used to read books for fun? Well, they might be reading *less* because of technology but they are listening *more* because of technology. As mentioned previously, the average amount of time a teenager spends listening to music is about 2.5 hours per day.

How can we use reading in Rhymecology? A simple, yet powerful, technique is to print up the lyrics to a song and read them with your client. During my workshops, I have noted that some of the most intense focus and participation comes from youth reading and deciphering lyrics to hip-hop songs.

Hip-hop beats are entrancing. Hip-hop beats get people to move their feet. Hip-hop beats can also be so powerful that listeners ignore the lyrics. Even those who *hear* the rap songs might not *listen* to them. When song lyrics are printed on a page and broken down line by line, they are so much more powerful (for good or for bad). The breakdown of lyrics allows us to critically analyze hip-hop lyrics and culture. When one is able to critically analyze this, it gives us the opportunity for one of the important Rhymecology goals: The demystification of hip-hop.

In the above quote from my poem "Hiphopisbadnowbutitwasgoodthen" I say that in "the first verse they have an iced out necklace, chain and rings". The image of diamond or gold necklaces is quite common in hip-hop. Then I say "But in the next verse their complaining they got no fame or cream (cash)". Many songs contradict themselves and when you are able to spot these with a client, it takes away some of the rappers power and gives some to the client.

One of the all time great rappers was the Notorious B.I.G. and one of his biggest hits was "Juicy". In the first verse he says

"I'm blowin' up like you thought I would/Call the crib, same number same hood," implying that he was a successful artist but he still was living the same way as he always has. In fact, he was in the same house with the same phone number. Now fast forward to the third verse in the same song,

"My whole crew is loungin'/Celebratin' every day, no more public housin'/Thinkin' back on my one-room shack/Now my mom pimps an Ack with minks on her back." This implies that he has moved out of his childhood house and is buying mink coats for his mother. So which one is it? Is he "keeping it real" by staying in his old neighborhood or is he so rich that the old neighborhood is a memory?.

> **When we read the lyrics it becomes apparent that like writer, actors, and news outlets, many hip-hop artists tell STORIES.**

Not all therapists will be able to understand the songs which clients play for them. Not all clients will understand the lyrics that the therapists play for them. Once "rap rapport" has been struck, it is essential to use this technique in sessions. This "Print Up" Technique should be used throughout your Rhymecology sessions and will be referenced throughout the guide. In each chapter I will provide song titles for you to look up (with your client or in-between sessions). When you find one that will resonate with your client, print the lyrics and bring to session.

RHYMECOLOGY® TECHNIQUE:

Ask your client what his/her favorite song is. Get the spelling of the artist and song. Search the internet for the lyrics and print them. Bring them to the next session and go through them with the client. Do not respond with any negatives. Give two positive comments and then ask a question. For example, "Wow this guy is really good at telling you how he feels", and "I can see how this is a popular song" before "I wonder what were the consequences from that decision".

You don't HAVE to ask therapeutic questions. Sometimes just reading through the lyrics and showing interest further develops your rap rapport and that is what we want!

"I'm tired of the state rap is in
90% of the shit rappers kick is subject matterless
Not original but blasphemous
A bunch of characters shooting the same videos, it's embarrassing"

-Canibus

8: THEMED THERAPY

Take a moment to visualize the themes which make up hip-hop music (No, really), (I'll wait...)

What were the initial images that come to your head? Were they violent? Sexual? Alcohol or drug related? If you thought of those images, you are right on. The truth is that you *should* think of those images because that is how hip-hop culture is most often portrayed by the media. (When I think of hip-hop I think of those images but I also think of poetry, passion, multi-syllabic rhyme schemes, alliteration, history, therapy, self-expression, teamwork, goal setting, ambition, love letters, journaling, dreams, frustration, joy, community, rage and unmatched creativity).

When hip-hop music started to seep from the inner cities into the suburbs there was an immediate concern from parents, educators and even politicians that the music was going to affect our youth in negative ways (Selfhout, Delsing, Bogt & Meeus 2008). Isn't it interesting: it became an issue when it hit the suburbs? Parents didn't want these "rap themes" in their home; the more they didn't want them, the more taboo it became and the more the youth *did* want them.

By the early 1990's people were relating to the themes in hip-hop music because they were going through the same hardships. At the same time there was a new legion of fans dipping their toes in hip-hop for a number of reasons: taboo, curiosity, rebellion, being cool etc. By 1993-1994 hip-hop music had become the voice of a generation and the themes were suddenly talking points across the United States.

Presidential candidate Dan Quayle said of Tupac Shakur's *2pacalypse Now,* "There is absolutely no reason for a record like this to be published by a responsible corporation…It has no place in our society." (*2pacalypse Now* makes it onto the Rhymecology® suggested listening list as the artist addressed teenage pregnancy, abortion and absent father figures). At the same time democratic power Tipper Gore was testifying to the ills of gangster rap.

How times have changed! In 2014, Republican Senator Marco Rubio spoke of the very same Tupac Shakur's music in glowing terms and said, "In some ways, rappers are like reporters. In particular, at that time, from the West Coast, it was a lot of reporting about what life was like … so the '90s was a time when this was really pronounced. You had gang wars, racial tension, and they were reporting on that." Rapper Jay-Z's songs stay on President Obama's Ipod because he "tells American stories".

Whether it is considered good or bad, hip-hop has weaved its way into nearly all facets of American life. So how can it not be a major part of therapy with urban adolescents?

The following are Rhymecology® techniques in which one can use the specific type of hip-hop to gain greater insight into your clients. Some of the sub genres of greatest concern in hip-hop include Gangster Rap, Self Medicating, Degradation, and Materialism. Use the following examples to turn those negatively perceived topics into healing points for you and your client.

*Disclaimer- Not all of the techniques apply or will work with clients who listen to these particular genres.

**Double Disclaimer- These ideas and techniques are based on my experience and my opinion.

"When I'm called off, I got a sawed off
Squeeze the trigger and bodies are hauled off
You too boy, if ya fuck with me
The police are gonna hafta come and get me
Off yo ass that's how I'm goin out
For the punk motherfuckers that's showin out..."
-N.W.A

9: GANGSTER RAP

Does your client listen to gangster rap that features lots of violence?

Gangster rap burst on to the scene in 1988 with the album *Straight Outta Compton* by the controversial group N.W.A. Talking about the subtleties of drug dealing, of police brutality, of prostitution and much more, so, of course, it was a huge success! Much of "gangsta" rap involves heavy cursing, disrespecting others and talking about killing. Sometimes the artist says that they are shooting people for money, sometimes they are rival gang members, sometimes for no reason at all. The artist is not actually committing the act of which they speak but only describing it on a record. But do your clients understand that?

It is important for clients to understand that most of the gangsta acts described are specifically because they have been proven to sell more records. Record label owners do not care about the effect on the community or youth. Artists are not always real "gangstas" and often times they are told to put on a persona in order to sell more records.

I was recently playing a song for a client of mine who wants to be a rapper. In it Eminem said *"I'm already wanted for sellin' keys/And bunch of other felonies from A to Z like spellin' bees/So before I dropped to the ground and fell on knees/ I bust shots, they bust back/Hit the square in the chest, he wasn't wearin' a vest"*. While my goal was to educate him on Eminem's complicated rhyme schemes, I hadn't taken into account the graphic detail of the story. But rather than turn the story off, I let it play until the end. The client's reaction was "Did he really do that??" Of course, the answer was no! I was able to explain that Eminem is a gifted story teller who was creating a story about a robbery gone bad which eventually led to a shootout with police. By playing the song "Murder, Murder" I was able to:

1) Gauge whether the client pays attention to the lyrics
2) Explain the fact that most rappers are storytellers (like filmmakers)
3) Follow how one bad decision (the robbery) can lead to prison or death (shootout)

When listening to hard core gangsta rap, these are all important listening/teaching points that must be portrayed to the client.

WHAT GANGSTA RAP MEANS

Rhymecology® calls the description of shooting someone in music, a sign of anger. In that moment where a rapper is talking about taking someone's life, he is in actuality taking his/her power back. He is standing tall, watching others fall. He is taking out his frustrations. He is winning.

Many of your clients don't feel empowered. They don't have reasonable places, ways or techniques to express their anger. When a gangster rapper does that for them *the listener is in alignment with that anger and they are taking their power back vicariously.* Gangster rappers present rage and a feeling of hopelessness and when our kids are listening to it, there are in accordance with those very feelings.

I am not a gangsta. I never held a gun or been gang affiliated. But when my anger reaches a boiling point, instead of screaming or talking to my therapist, I often put on Gangsta Rap. LOUD. I have all the skills and techniques to self-soothe. I am a master meditator. I deep breathe with the best of them. But there are times, when nothing else will do except listening to gangsta rap.

It is important to let your client enjoy his/her gangster rap and to understand what they feel when they listen to it. You might want to tell them that listening to music is a great thing to do when one is frustrated or angry.

A few examples of classic gangsta rap songs follow:

*"Straight Outta Compton"- N.W.A

"My Summer Vacation"- Ice Cube

"Boyz in Da Hood"- Eazy E

"Shook Ones II"- Mobb Deep

"High Rollers"- Ice-T

RHYMECOLOGY®TECHNIQUE:

Ask him/her to write either in poem form, rhyme form or through just journaling about what makes them angry.

If it seems too much like "therapy" for a client, ask them to write from the persona of their favorite gangsta rapper. "What do would your favorite rapper say if he was feeling like you are right now?"

Often they need encouragement by example. Take a piece of paper and write at the top of it. "I get so pissed off when..." and self-disclose a few fun facts about yourself. Then write it on his/her page and ask them to do the same.

"I get really PISSED (angry/mad) when..."

10. SELF MEDICATING

"Let's smoke that bowl, hit the bong
And then take that finger off of that hole
Plug it, unplug it, don't strain
I love you Mary Jane" -Cypress Hill

Does your client listen to party rap filled with lots of drinking and marijuana smoking?

Rappers have never had a problem describing their favorite drinks, from malt liquor to champagne; their choice of alcohol makes it into many verses. There have also been countless (no, literally, COUNTless) rappers who use their albums as a platform to talk about their affection for marijuana. Often the artists just mention marijuana in passing but there are also certain artists who make drinking or smoking the primary focus of their rhymes.

Rappers are not the first artists with substance abuse issues. From Billie Holiday, to Bob Marley, to the Beatles, drug references in music have spawned generations and genres. Even with that, people seem to point the finger at hip-hop. It should be noted that in most cases, emcees don't talk about using harder or psychedelic drugs. In fact, **hip-hop pioneers often used their songs as a platform for anti-drug messages**.

That being said, there are not many "anti" drug emcees in the current state of hip-hop. This makes it all the more important to educate clients on songs like the ones mentioned above. Rappers are act like it is legal and so does the current generation. The Center of Addiction and Substance Abuse report that 70% of youth age fifteen to seventeen reports that drugs are either used sold or kept at their schools. Combine that with the fact that perceived idols (athletes/movie stars/musicians) are being busted for using more often than creating anti-drug ads, it is obvious we must discuss this with clients. What better way than by using hip-hop?

Archives of Pediatrics and Adolescent Medicine state that one in three popular songs contain explicit references to drugs and or alcohol and that 77% of popular rap songs contain those explicit references to substance use. If a teenage client is listening to 2.5 hours of music per day, that makes 251 unsupervised references to substance abuse per day.

WHAT SELF MEDICATING HIP-HOP MEANS

While the number of artists who promote marijuana use is uncountable, there are some who make it their main lyrical focus. You will find out which type of artist your client is listening to. If it is the artists who focus on partying, it is probable that your client is self medicating also. So what does it mean?

Current rap artists who smoke lots of weed and let you know about it include:

Wiz Khalifa

    Snoop Dogg

        Action Bronson

            School Boy Q

                Rick Ross

When people self-medicate they are trying to escape their current reality. It is the same when they are listening to songs about getting high. It feels better to be stoned, high or listening to songs about it than it is to be sober. More often than not at a young impressionable age, fans of drinking and smoking rap are going to at the very least experiment with that path, if they have not already.

You want to have enough rapport with a client so that they can talk to you about drinking or doing drugs. If a client is known to self medicate, why not use hip-hop to tackle the issue head on. The following are hip-hop songs which strongly promote the use of drugs and alcohol. All could be used as a catalyst to a deeper discussion with self-medicating clients.

* "Drug Ballad"- Eminem

"Reefer Party"- Wiz Khalifa

"Because I got High"- Afroman

"Hits from the Bong"- Cypress Hill

It is true that the above songs promote heavy marijuana smoking but I guarantee you these are the type of songs which your self-medicating clients listen to. Don't avoid them. Once you explore them with your client, then you can open the discussion to *anti*-drug songs. Such as:

"Slow Down"- Brand Nubian

* "Dan The Man"- J.Walker & Gilli Moon

"Prescription/Oxymoron"- ScHoolBoy Q

"Night of the Living Baseheads"- Public Enemy

"White Lines (Don't Do It)"- Grandmaster Flash

RHYMECOLOGY® TECHNIQUE

Ask client to write either in poem form, rhyme form or through journaling about the difference the client feels when he or she is self medicating as opposed to going through the day sober. Possible titles are "Why I get High", "Its Better High", or "Sobriety Sucks because".

Ask him/her to write a story or song about what are the possible outcomes for someone (not them of course) who becomes addicted to drugs.

11. DEGREDATION

"I could give you a bitch and wouldn't give you a joint
Bitches ain't shit and now I made my point"
-Too Short

Does your client listen to lyrics which degrade and disrespect women?

One of the most controversial issues in hip-hop has been the degrading names which they call their women and the bragging on the sexual acts which they enact with these women. While this has slightly decreased over the years, it is still very common to hear a rapper refer to women as "bitches". Rappers will argue that they are not referring to *all* women but only the ones who deserve to called that. For reference to this, check the song "Wonder Why They Call You Bitch" by Tupac. Nonetheless, the careless usage of these words has made its way into the vocabulary of pre-teenagers across the world. While walking by clusters of children, I often here 6th grade boys referring to their 6th grade girls as "Bitches".

The number of rappers who use lyrics to degrade are much higher than the number who respect women. This does not mean that there are not scores of positive males who love and respect their women. That is one of the reasons you have this guide! Use it to show off the hip-hop songs which promote love, inspiration, respect, joy and family (many examples of these songs and artists are sprinkled throughout the guide). Here, in fact, use these:

"Womenology"- KRS-One

"Keep Ya Head Up"- Tupac

* "Black Girl Pain"- Talib Kweli

"For Women"- Talib Kweli

"The Light"- Common

When pop culture idols are disrespectful it filters into the consciousness of the youth. Clients I have worked with in lower SES environments have become accustomed to hearing rappers degrading them. Use (and print) the above songs with female clients who might need to hear positive things said about them.

There are so many different themes in hip-hop music. If a male client is choosing to listen to songs which focus mainly on degrading women, we have look at what is behind that. Look at the relationship between a client and his mother. If the client is being raised by a grandmother, group home or foster care, then they are lacking the main mother figure in their world. If there is abuse or neglect in that home then it is likely there is anger and most teenagers don't know how to handle anger or hatred towards their mother. Can you see how unprocessed anger towards their mother figure can be reinforced by hip-hop songs which degrade women?

Clients who have good relationships with their mother figures are going to have less anger towards women and hence will then not gravitate to these types of artists and lyrics. If a client is constantly listening to rap songs using and degrading women, it might be a signal that he has unresolved anger towards his/her mother figure.

RHYMECOLOGY® TECHNIQUE:

1) Ask client to write either in poem form, rhyme form or through just journaling about what kind of relationship he or she would like to be in when they turn thirty years old. Is it a positive one of nurturing and love or is it one of using and abusing (like their songs are saying). Ask them to really "feel" what they want. This should take a little bit of the power away from the song.

2) Ask client to write either in poem form, rhyme form or through just journaling about their relationship with important female figures in their life. Mother, grandmother, teacher etc. Is there a similar theme?

"Waiting for The Lord to rise

I look into my daughter's eyes

 And realize I'm going to learn through her"

- Common

12. WHO YOU CALLIN A BITCH?

Newsflash. There are great female emcees. There are female rappers who keep their clothes on and can rap as well or better than any male rappers. They don't get the credit, the marketing or the money that men do in this business. Since the mid 1990's female emcees who've gained mainstream notoriety did it by booty shaking (save Lauryn Hill). Because of that youth today are not aware that there were and are great female emcees In fact, since I have your attention, I'm going to share a short story.

I was sitting in my car with a sixteen year old Hispanic client. A pretty girl, she had already had had a few boyfriends. Numerous times she has had peers either in school or in the neighborhood grab her behind or even kiss her without invitation. She also had been molested, called a "bitch", "slut" and worse. She had recently shared (during Rap Rapport building) that she liked rapper Lil Wayne who is quoted with such fine lyrics as "acting like I'm him and fuck the best nigga, I AM bitches wanna fuck like they're me and I'm them yeaa, they share me like oxygen". I didn't judge because I know (and you do to now) that these type of lyrics are more accessible than the type I recommend. I mentioned to her that Lil Wayne says that he doesn't write, as in he is illiterate. I told her I knew his songs but that his constant drug, alcohol and sexual rhymes bore me now that I am older. I pulled out an old scratched up CD by Queen Latifah and put on the 1990 song "U.N.I.T.Y." The client knew Latifah from movies and T.V. shows but did not know she was a rapper. I just let it play.

Instinct leads me to another flow
Everytime I hear a brother call a girl a bitch or a ho
Trying to make a sister feel low
You know all of that gots to go
Now everybody knows there's exceptions to this rule
Now don't be getting mad, when we playing, it's cool
But don't you be calling out my name
I bring wrath to those who disrespect me like a dame
That's why I'm talking, one day I was walking down the block
I had my cutoff shorts on right cause it was crazy hot
I walked past these dudes when they passed me
One of 'em felt my booty, he was nasty
I turned around red, somebody was catching the wrath
Then the little one said (Yeah me bitch) and laughed
Since he was with his boys he tried to break fly
Huh, I punched him dead in his eye and said "Who you calling a bitch?"

I peeked through corner of my eye and saw my client smiling, BIG!

She said "I can see how this was popular". Latifah's lyrics were clear and powerful and held a message. The name calling and butt grabbing paralleled my client's own experiences, so imagine how gratifying it felt for when Latifah "punched him dead in his eye and said 'Who you calling a bitch?'" My client said "I have never heard a female stand up for herself like that."

Those of us with young female clients have a responsibility to educate them on powerful female voices. In a sexist, male dominated industry there have been a number of female emcee standouts. However, they rarely if ever get the marketing which often less talented men get. I am providing a list of artists and albums which you can share with your female clients. I recommend all of these albums for not only female clients but for people who love great hip-hop.

Queen Latifah- *Black Reign*

* Lauryn Hill- *The Miseducation of Lauryn Hill*

MC Lyte- *Lyte as a Rock, Ain't No Other*

Rapsody- *Beauty and the Beast*

Jean Grae- *Blue Sky Black Death*

In the Ferrari or Jaguar switchin four lanes
With the top down screamin out
Money ain't a thang
Bubble hard in the double R flashin the rings
With the window cracked holler back
Money ain't a thang
Jigga, I don't like it if it don't gleam clean
And to hell with the price
cause the money ain't a thang

- Jay-Z

13. MATERIALISM

The violent and misogynistic messages pale in comparison to theme of materialism which has inundated hip-hop. Until I began working in the inner-cities of Los Angeles I didn't understand the effect that materialist rap was having on youth. My clients are primarily African American and Latino but there have been a number of white clients as well. I have had both male and female clients. Their ages have ranged from 3 to 17. The one thing they all have in common is that their SES (socioeconomic status) is very poor. And most of them want to be rappers.

And why not? Rappers make it seem like being a rapper is so easy. Just write some rhymes (or have them written for you), lay down songs, drink, smoke, have lots of sex and make lots of money. *Take a moment to imagine how that would feel.* Then imagine how it would feel for an inner city child who has not been afforded the opportunities others have and who has not been provided a proper education about finances.

The cycle is real. Urban youth who grow up poor want what they see as success, which is normally money, jewelry or cars. Nobody tells them differently so they are under the impression that if they can get those things, they have made it. Rappers are told by the record labels to keep rapping about money, jewels and cars because "that is what the kids want to hear". Kids become adults, maybe rappers themselves, and what do you think they are going to rap about? The cycle continues.

What would it be like if rappers bragged about how much money they are saving? What about the investment they made in that startup company which turned out to be gold mine? What if rappers made songs about the happy home they created with their spouse as a result of their songs? What if our youth was inundated with *those* messages?

Unfortunately, there are not many artists who rap about their 401K. As artist Dante Stubbs puts it, "Most rappers, including myself, come from nothing, like poverty, broken homes or abuse. So when they start making money, that's what they want to talk about since they never had it before."

It can be said that the odds becoming a successful rapper are much lower than becoming a successful doctor. Most of us know a friend who is a doctor but how many people personally know successful, mainstream rappers who have made a living from their songwriting for more than a decade? Damn. I should have been a doctor. But then again I wouldn't be writing this guide about my two favorite topics. I digress.

Music in general has always been an outlet to effectively convey a struggle, be it related to family, work, love, abuse or failed ambitions. Socioeconomic hardships clearly fall into that "struggle" category and, thus, are food for lyrics to which a broad base of people will easily relate. But sometimes, when the listener comes from a world outside of the socioeconomic realm from which the genre was born, it becomes harder to understand (or easier to misinterpret) the connotations and message.

The following songs are all different creative interpretations of rappers lust/need/passion for money. Each song could be introduced in session to delve deeper into a client's psyche.

* "Money is my Bitch"- Nas

"C.R.E.A.M (Cash Rules Everything Around Me)"- Wu Tang Clan

"Money, Power, Respect"- The L.O.X.

"I Love the Dough"- Notorious B.I.G featuring Jay-Z

* "Money Ain't a Thang"- Jay-Z & Jermaine Dupri

I suggest each of these songs as they will play upon different feelings in each client. As far as suggesting one song which encompasses the inner city mind set and how dangerous "quick money" can be, please look into:

"Love's Gonna Getcha"- Boogie Down Productions

This is a beautifully crafted song/story about an inner city adolescent who starts selling drugs to improve his family's financial situation. It paints the picture from his point of view and then shows the dangers of that lifestyle and ultimately how dangerous it is can be to fall in love with material things.

(WATCH THE VIDEO & PRINT THE LYRICS TO THIS!)

RHYMECOLOGY® TECHNIQUE:

1) Ask client to write either in poem form, rhyme form or through just journaling about how much better things would be if money was not an issue. How would it "feel" to have the money they desire? What would they do with that money? Then ask what they are willing to do to GET that money?

14. THE GOLDEN ERA

I thought the ghetto was the worst that could happen to me
I'm glad I listened when my father was rappin to me
Cuz back in the day they lived in caves
Exhiled from the original man, they strayed away
Now that's what I call hard times
I'd rather be here to exercise the mind."
–Eric B & Rakim

Okay ya'll, let me get on my soap box here for a minute. This is going to be the "Everything was better in my generation" chapter. While that may not be true in all aspects, when it comes to hip-hop, I can say that it most certainly was.

The "Golden Era" of hip-hop ranges from roughly 1987 to 1993 (historians differ by a year or two each way). I was an impressionable young person during these years, so I am biased and admittedly have nostalgia about the era. With that said, let me explain why it is the best and why young fans need to know about it.

Creativity

The golden era was extremely innovative. As put by Rolling Stone Magazine, "it seemed that every new single reinvented the genre". Writer William Jelani Cobb says "what made the era they inaugurated worthy of the term golden was the sheer number of stylistic innovations that came into existence... in these golden years, a critical mass of mic prodigies were literally creating themselves and their art form at the same time".

DJ's and producers began to sample records in ways not seen before or since. Sampling is defined "the act of taking a portion, or sample, of one sound recording and reusing it as an instrument or a sound recording in a different song or piece." Artists were sampling jazz, funk, rock and roll and even movies. Legendary Wu-Tang producer the RZA sampled his home collection of kung fu movies to add an authentic feel to the Wu songs. Strict laws and guidelines would prevent him from doing that in today's music business. The Beastie Boys sampled 24 different songs on "B-Boy Bouillabaisse"!

When it came to the art of rapping, the golden era provided so many advances that 30 years later some rappers are still catching up. Artists such as Big Daddy Kane, Rakim and Kool G. Rap all took rhyming to new levels. Multiple syllable rhymes, inner sentence rhyming, alliteration, word play and the heavy use of metaphors and similes all came into play…in every song!

The Message

Not only were they wizards with the words, hip hop was also becoming a form of social protest. Rhymes from the Golden Era often drew attention to a variety of social issues including Afrocentric living, drug use, crime and violence, religion, culture, the state of the American economy, as well as, the modern man's struggle. Emcees of the era were reporting on the state of the inner city in creative powerful ways that had never been heard before. They were providing the truth while at the same time <u>pushing themselves and their community to be better</u>. The selected quote by Rakim at the start of the chapter talks about the hardship of the ghetto, listening to his father, perspective hard times and the importance of using his mind...all in 6 lines. One of the great all time songs (in my opinion), Rakim tells us how "*I learn to relax in my room and escape from New York/and return through the womb of the world as a thought*". Here is a young black man using his voice to tell his listeners that he taught himself a coping technique, which is essentially mindfulness or meditation.

The golden era emcees were not perfect and there are exceptions to everything in this chapter. But the majority of emcees all had a sound distinct to the region; they reported on what people of the region were going through, rather than what a marketing specialist told them to. When most emcees talked about money, it was motivating. The message was "we can do better". When those emcees bragged of having some money it was only a part of their overall concept. The current commercialization of hip-hop pushes the rich rapper image to the extreme and mainstream rappers spend a majority of their raps bragging about being rich. They took the image but left out the hard work and the emotion out. Underground rapper Immortal Technique said it so well, "I pledge no allegiance, fuck the presidents speeches/what the industry did to Pac, they did to Jesus/raping his vocals then destroying his message..."

In the early 20th century, African American communities a music genre called jazz; it became one of America's original art forms. The genius of jazz music was that it didn't need a voice and some of greatest jazz musicians were African Americans who let the instruments do the talking. Slavery and segregation were not "legally" present in the mid 1980's but mainstream media culture was still dominated by white males. Incredible athletes in the early 1980s were still coached and played on teams owned by white men. When hip-hop began, DJs were the neighborhood stars. Breakdancers and graffiti artists were also well known. None of them were used their voice. There was still no voice of black America.

Hip-hop gave black America a voice at a time when it was needed. That is why the Golden Era emcees (notice I say emcees, not rappers) were so crucial to a culture, a generation, a people. These emcees represented the African American struggle of so many generations while at the same time paving the path for future ones. This could be why so many emcees rapped with such passion not only about the culture and black pride but also about their community and the children in it. These emcees broke the choke hold of white mainstream America which in turn allowed someone like Jay-Z to own his own record label and clothing line and all that followed.

The next segment will provide a number of samples of Golden Era hip-hop. These selections have been powerful with a number of my African American clients.

Eric B & Rakim- * "In The Ghetto"

Mind keeps traveling, I'll be back after I
Stop and think about the brothers and sisters in Africa
Return the thought through the eye of a needle
For miles I thought and I just fought the people
Under the dark skies on a dark side
Not only there but right here's an apartheid
So now is the time for us to react
Take a trip through the mind and when you get back
Understand you're third eye seen all of that
It ain't where you're from, it's where you're at

Public Enemy- "Brothers Gonna Work it Out"

Look here, not a thing to fear
Brother to brother not another as sincere
Teach a man how to be father
To never tell a woman he can't bother
You can't say you don't know
What I'm talkin' 'bout
But one day ... brothers gonna work it out

EPMD- "The Crossover"

Some say, "There's no business like show business,"
But if that's the truth, please explain why is this:
Rap has been around long, makin' mad noise you see
Still I haven't seen one rapper livin' comfortably
No time to pick and wish on a four leaf clover
I stick to underground, keep the crossover

Jungle Brothers- "Black is Black"

I try, try to tell my people
We all are one, created equal
Before we master we must plan
Is that so hard to understand?
Today's the day we get together
To try to change and make things better
If not where will be be tomorrow?
Drownin in a pool of sorrow
Daylight shines but still few see
That we must fight for unity
In a picture that's fixed as black and white
Why's it both that have to fight?
Uplift the race, uplift the race
See my soul and not my face
All for one and one for all

Big Daddy Kane- "Young, Gifted and Black"

Ashes to ashes and dust to dust
So understand, the way that I live
That's positive - and the message I got to give
It's a benefit for you and me
I'm talkin bout P.E.A.C.E
The chosen one that has turned a new leaf
I got gold teeth, and they don't chew beef
No pork on my fork, strictly fish on my dish
The Kane fallin victim?? Sucker, you wish!

Lord Finesse- "A Lesson to be Taught"

I'm not trying to diss you or even teach you
But here to teach you we are all equal
And show y'all in fact there's a better way
Than depending on Welfare or Medicaid
So finish up school and pass the scholar quiz
And show your children what the value of a dollar is
Cause many children are hard to please today
Cause they're searching for some type of easy way
But there's not, so who's at fault here?
So think about the lesson being taught here
How many brothers in the world you see today
Can say that they're living the legal way?

Is there anybody you know that could use messages like these?
If so, look up these songs and play them with your client!

KRS-ONE –
Knowledge Reigns Supreme Over Nearly Everyone

Goodie MOB – the Good Die Mostly Over Bullshit

Big Daddy KANE – King Asiatic, Nobody's Equal

GURU – Gifted Unlimited Rhymes Universal

B.I.B.L.E- Basic Instructions Before Leaving Earth

R.E.B.I.R.T.H-
Real Emcees Bring Intelligent Rhymes to Hip-Hop

15. ALLIES IN ACRONYMS

There are many subliminal messages which can be transferred into the minds of our youth through lyrics. As previously discussed, one of those themes is the negative name calling, especially of women. It is possible to change the way your clients look at the words/names themselves.

Ask your female clients if they like to think of themselves as those names (slut, bitch, hoe etc). Tell them that they can either allow themselves to take on the negative energy surrounding those names OR they can change it completely by using acronyms as allies.

What if every time they heard the word "Bitch" on a song they thought of the woman Being In Total Control Herself? After hearing this empowering Acronym, I came up with a few more.

Have your client memorize each of these acronyms and then replace the meaning when the words come up in songs or in their day to day life.

They could even create their own!

S L U T = Smart Likeable Understanding Together

W H O R E = Woman Holding Only Real Essence

H O E = Handle On Everything

F A G = Fun Awesome Guy

N E R D = Never Ever Really Down

C U N T = Caring Understanding Nobodies Tramp

"Got more soul than a sock with a hole"

16. SIMILES & METAPHOR MAGIC

A great warm-up Rhymecology® exercise to use with your client is Metaphor Magic. It is simple and effective. The reason we use this is that it is a safe warm up that also kick starts both the client and the therapist into a creative writing mode.

Begin the exercise by explaining that all of the truly talented hip-hop lyricists are masters of the similes and metaphors. It would even be hard to name great songs or artists in hip-hop who DON'T use them well.

Rappers use the literary techniques of double entendres, alliteration, and other forms of wordplay that are also found in classical poetry. Similes and metaphors are used extensively in rap lyrics; rappers such as Fabolous and Lloyd Banks have written entire songs in which every line contains similes, whereas MCs like Rakim, GZA, and Jay-Z are known for the metaphorical content of their raps. Lil Wayne is also known for his frequent use of similes and metaphors. English teachers could use the following examples when teaching similes and metaphors. In fact they should, right?

:

"I drop the greats like clumsy waiters drop plates." –Mr. Mann

"I'm a dirty rotten rhymer/ cursing at you players worse than Marty Schottenheimer."- Eminem

"I'm the Michael Jordan of rap."- Jay-Z

"I keep one eye open like CBS"- Jay-Z

"I hold the microphone like a grudge."- Rakim

"I'm cooler than a polar bear's toenails... bend corners like I was a curve, I struck a nerve." –Outkast

"To the British im ghandi, to the japanese im an american pilot flying over Nagasaki, to the aids patient im your last antibody waiting for a cure from modern biology"
- Canibus

"Like a circle of knives, I got the sharpest flow around"- Lil Wayne

"I'm intellectual, pass more essays, than motor police parades through east L.A."- Pharoahe Monch

*My rhymes are like shot clocks,
interstate cops
and blood clots,
my point is your flow gets stopped.*- Talib Kweli

"Just because I stand over you doesn't mean you understand me."- Immortal Technique

"...cuz all my jewels be rocky like sylvester stallone" – Big L

"I got a question, as serious as cancer" -Rakim

RHYMECOLOGY® TECHNIQUE

I'm hot like _____

I'm cold like _____

I'm tall like _____

I'm smart like _____

My house is like a _____

I'm hungrier than _____

I'm as lonely as a _____

My brain is like a _____

I will be as rich as _____

I am a leader just like _____

This can either be used strictly as a warm up or the answers can be used in future rhymes. Let's pretend that your client said that "I'm hot like the sun" or "I'm hot as the sun". A word like "sun" could easily be rhymed with. How many can you think of?

bun, done, fun, gun, hun, none, nun, one, pun, run, son, ton

With all the above words at your disposal, can you see how we can create a little rhyme with a nice simile? If the client needs a little bit of prodding, it is up to you to lead the client.

"Maybe do you want to make money by the ton?"

"Have you ever had anybody call you hun?'"

"What do you do for fun?"

These are questions you can ask to get the ball rolling. Then take their answer and combine it with the simile or metaphor and just like that you have two good lines that rhyme!

"My girlfriend is the only one calls me hun/ she says I'm hot as the sun."

"I'm hot like the sun/ want to make money by the ton."

You may want to rearrange some of the questions to fit your particular client. For example, if you know your client is not lonely at all, you would not use the "I'm as lonely as" fill in.. Make it fit for your particular client. Do the exercise with all of the above similes and metaphors (plus any others you can think of) and you are off to a good start with hip-hop therapy.

18. RHYMECOLOGY® EXERCISES

The mission statement of Rhymecology® is to use the power of hip-hop lyrics to help as many people as possible express, discover and create themselves. In the previous section we discussed how listening to hip-hop can give you insight into your client's world. In this section I will give examples of Rhymecology® exercises.

This is My Song

The key is to sit with your client, one-on-one, and talk to them. I usually ask, "Have you seen any pictures of yourself when you were a *kid*? Seems like a long time ago doesn't it? Well, today we are going to create something that you can look back on in ten years and you will say 'Oh my, I am so glad I wrote that back when I was fifteen. I was so young then.' Basically we want to create a photograph of your life."

Ask the client:

His/her name and age

Favorite food

Favorite music

Favorite things to do

Who they live with

One thing they love

One Thing they hate

One thing that is interesting about themselves

It is important to use non-threatening questions in this exercise. The answers will vary for each client. Let's just say that your client's name is **Jon,** and he is **15 years old**. His favorite food is **Mexican food.** His favorite music is **Rap.** He likes to play **video games**. He lives in a **group home**. One thing he loves is **skateboarding** and one thing he hates is **school**. Something interesting is that he has **lived in ten group homes**/foster homes.

Write down the key words (bolded above) and some words that rhyme with them. If you have no idea what rhymes with **Jon** write down the alphabet on top of the page.

A B C D E F G H I J K L M N O P Q R S T U V W X Z Y

Replace the 'J' in Jon with each letter in the alphabet and frenetically come up with rhymes (or at least something close!)

Bomb. Con. Don. Gone. Kong. Long. Lawn. Song. Strong. Wrong.

Be sure to ask your client (in this case Jon) which word *he* wants to use.

Next, help the client fill in the sentences. We have the name **Jon** and a bunch of words that rhyme with his name. A perfect introduction line could be, "My name is Jon (or whatever the name is) and this is my song!" Once you begin writing it is important to use your observation skills and what you know of your client to create the rhyme. Maybe Jon is on the football team, possibly a big guy. Look at the possible words above. What could you use?

"My name is Jon, this is my song/ They say I am strong as King Kong".

He is 15. So what rhymes with "teen"? Go to the alphabet, replace the first letter and sound it out! Possible rhymes for teen:

Been. **D**ean. **F**iend. **G**reen. **J**eans. **K**een. **M**ean. **L**ean. **S**cene. **W**ean.

Which word can you associate with Jon. Ask him. Maybe his favorite color is "green". Maybe he likes to wear Levi "Jeans". Or... maybe, just maybe he doesn't like it when his caregiver is "mean"? Do you see how we can just stumble into some therapeutic bits in a roundabout way?

"My name is Jon this is my song/ They say I am strong as King Kong/ Right now I am only fifteen/ I never make a scene cuz she can be mean... "

Jon said that he likes to skateboard. I would use the verb "Skating" here and plug it in. Again visit the alphabet, change the first letter of Skating and sound out the possibilities.

Dating. **F**aking. **H**ating. **M**aking. **R**ating. **T**aking. **W**aiting.

Again, be sure to ask your client which word he wants to use. Once he picks the word, together you can create a sentence. I suggest keeping it simple. A common term used when kids talk bad about each other is, "hating" and is used in rap often.

"My name is Jon this is my song/ They say I am strong as King Kong/ Right now I am only fifteen/ I never make a scene cuz she can be mean/ My favorite thing to do is skating/ It keeps me away from people that are hating..."

In a short amount of time you have come up with a half a poem/rap which is cool, creative and introspective. In some cases your client will be able to think of rhymes quickly, in some cases you will have to literally write the sentences for him. It just doesn't matter how it gets done. The key is to keep this <u>light and fun</u> and to give your client **all** the credit for creating it.

19. FOCUS TOPIC

Similar to "This is My Song", the goal is to gather whatever information the client wants to share and create rhymes with it. The difference is that you should hone in on one topic and try to explore the details, thoughts and feelings about that one topic. The example here will be every kid's favorite topic: School.

Use your same open ended questions to start.

"How long have you been going to school?"

"How does it make you feel when you do well in class?"

"How does it make you feel when you fail a test?"

"Do you think school is important? Why or why not?"

Let's say that the answers of those questions reveal that the client is a freshman in high school. She is a 'C' student who does not have many friends. She hates it when she fails. The few tests that she passed went unnoticed and unrewarded by her mother. After probing questions she reluctantly states that school is important because "It can help you get a job, I guess".

Again, we put down the alphabet on top of the page

A B C D E F G H I J K L M N O P Q R S T U V W X Z Y

It is important to look at the words the client gives you and have "back up words" as well. For example, if you can't think of a word that rhymes with freshman, use ninth grade or grade nine. Don't become stuck on the word that is in front of you! If you and your client cannot think of a rhyme, think of a similar or easier word!

"My name is Jayne, people say I am pretty plain/ I am in the ninth grade/ one day I hope I can get paid/ that is why I stay in school/ so I don't end up like a fool/ but when I do good they don't notice/ so it is hard to keep my focus/ and these girls act like little whores/ maybe it will get better as a sophomore".

99% of commercially successful songs have some sort of rhyming pattern and if your client ever wanted to make a song (or is an avid music listener) then these rhyming techniques will be a great tool. However, it is possible that your client (or you) may not be able to come up with rhymes to save your life. <u>It doesn't matter!</u> The same techniques could be used to create conventional poetry which does not have to rhyme. This could turn into a spoken word piece where the client expresses their rage while holding a blank piece of paper. It could turn into a love song about a boy they wish to meet in school The key to the Rhymecology® Focus Topics is open ended questions with a little bit of probing! I have given you the alphabet technique as a way to assist with rhyme creation. If however you are able to go online with the client while creating this, a great site is <u>www.rhymezone.com</u> or if you are using a phone the best app is called <u>Rhymers Block.</u> Simply type in the word and press enter. Rhyming words will come up! This is a helpful tool if your client wants to work on his/her rhyme by alone at home. There are also Rhyming Dictionaries which can be purchased inexpensively.

The Rhymecology® Focus Topics can be used for anything from a client's favorite ice cream to the client's abuse history. Start out with "This is My Song" then move on to easier general topics like school, food or games, then gently move into the reason they are in therapy!

EVEN THOUGH YOU'RE FED UP

YOU GOTTA KEEP YOUR HEAD UP.

-TUPAC SHAKUR

A B C D E F G H I J K L M N O P Q R S T U V W X Y Z

RHYMECOLOGY® WORKSHEET

Use the space below to write down three things: One that you love, one that you hate and something you DREAM of doing one day.

_____

_____

_____

Pick the one thing that you are feeling most <u>strongly</u> about today. Now write down all the feelings you associate with that thing. Write down WORDS that you associate with that thing. Write down the reasons why you feel so strongly about that particular thing. Don't think too much, just feel and write the words!

Using the alphabet find as many rhymes for the words above as you can.

RHYMECOLOGY® WORKSHEET pg 2

The difficult part is <u>done</u>! Now take your rhymes and *explain why* you love that thing, why you hate that thing or what you dream to do one day (if you can't do it in rhyme form, it's okay, just express yourself in any way you can!)

_____

_____

_____

_____

_____

_____

_____

_____

_____

_____

_____

_____

_____

_____

_____

_____

_____

_____

20. THE PROPHET PARAGRAPH

I leap over lies in a single bound (Who are you?)

The Black Prophet

One day I got struck by Knowledge of Self

It gave me super-scientifical powers

Now I, run through the ghetto

Battlin my, arch nemesis Mr. Ignorance

He's been tryin to take me out since the days of my youth

He feared this day would come

I'm hot on his trail, but sometimes he slips away

Because he has an army, they always give me trouble

Mainly - Hatred, Jealousy and Envy they attack me

They think they got me

But I use my super-science and I twist all three

I see sparks over that buildin - they're shootin at me

I dip, do a backflip

Then hit em in the heart with sharp steel bookmarks

Ignorance hates when I drop it

But no matter, what he do… he can't stop the Prophet- Jeru The Damaja

Get a hold of the song "You Can't Stop the Prophet" by Jeru the Damaja. It is on the album *The Sun Rises in the East.* In this song the emcee is personifying himself as a superhero in the inner city. But rather than fighting crime he is fighting against ignorance (as well as hatred, jealousy, anger, despair, deceit and more).

RHYMECOLOGY® EXERCISE:

Ask your client to identify yourself as an inner city hero and create a poem, rap, song, short story about it. If they had superpowers, what would they fight against, how and why?

_____

_____

_____

_____

_____

_____

_____

_____

_____

_____

_____

_____

_____

_____

21. PART TIME MUTHA EXERCISE

Some exercises are surface as we are creating rap rapport. Some get deep. The following exercise should only be used if you feel like the client is able to discuss trauma. The song is "Part Time Mutha" by Tupac on the album *2pacalapyse Now*. The song touches on topics such as single mothers, mothers on drugs, incest, unwanted pregnancy, rape, urban parenthood and more. The following verse is recited by Angelique. If you have a client who was raped/molested (especially by a family member) and they have been open enough to talk to you about it, consider this song as tool to help facilitate deeper discussion.

I only provide this verse as I have never heard a rap verse like it. The self disclosure of these taboo and shaming topics, combined with the power of her delivery, make this the most powerful verse I have heard.

(Again, do NOT use this until trust has been firmly cemented between you and the client or it seems like this would be helpful.)

"I grew up in a home where no-one liked me
Moms would hit the pipe, every night, she would fight me
Poppa was a nasty old man, like the rest
He's feeling on my chest, with his hand in my dress
Just another pest, and yes I was nervous

Blood sensor tests, I just don't deserve this

I wanna tell mom, but would she listen

She's bound to be bitchin if she hasn't got a fix in

So... now I lay me down to sleep

Lord don't let him rape me

If he does my soul to keep

Don't let the devil take me

Can't concentrate I contemplate in my classroom

Thinkin how my step dad, raped me in the bathroom

Every day I make class, and yet I'm missing periods

The thought of pregnancy is in my head and now I'm fearing it

I gotta tell mom, before she sees me

I told her how he G'd me, and she didn't believe me

Callin me a slut cuz my butt's kinda big so

Still that ain't no way to be talkin to your kids though

I can't believe the way you call it

Gotta believe in him, and dissin her own daughter

Time for me to break and find another

That's when I discovered

The ways of the days of a part time mutha"

22. HOW TO USE THE SKILLZ PROJECT

The following is a suggestion on how one could use the educational/therapeutic tool called the Skillz, written and recorded by the author of this guide, yours truly Jeff Walker aka J.Walker (If you don't' have the CD you can find it at www.skillzcd.com or search "J.Walker Skillz on iTunes).

I constantly hear about "conscious" or "positive" rappers. When I research them I often find that they have a few verses or maybe a few songs with somewhat positive messages. It is not enough! Even if they do create a positive album, you won't hear mental health issues addressed. So I wrote and recorded this album with a singular focus: To make a mental health hip-hop album which contained positive (and/or thought provoking) topics from the beginning to end.

My suggestion is to listen to each song and then discuss the message of each. The following pages contain prompts which can be a catalyst for discussions. If you purchase the hard copy of the CD (some people still do!) it comes with all of the lyrics printed in the booklet. The spaces are provided in case you wish to copy these pages and share with others.

Song 1 Skillz Intro

Have you ever done something because you heard a rapper say that THEY do it, in a song? If so, what was it and why did you do it?

_____

_____

_____

_____

_____

_____

Do you think that your parents understand hip-hop? Why or why not?

_____

_____

_____

_____

_____

_____

Why would parents want to keep their parents away from certain kinds of rap? Is that fair?

_____

_____

_____

_____

What would you do if you had a seven year old son that was listening to a song that said "Life ain't nothing but bitches and money?"

_____

_____

_____

_____

_____

_____

Song 2. It's Cool to Be Smart

What are the artists saying about school?

a) School is for suckers

b) Good grades can get you street cred

c) Don't be ashamed of intelligence, chances are it will pay off in the end

What is the most difficult part about school?

_____

_____

_____

Why would you want to do well in school? Why wouldn't you want to do well in school?

_____

_____

_____

_____

Why would the artist say "When you get older it's just the opposite, it actually pays to be a college kid"?

_____

_____

_____

_____

_____

Do you think it is possible to get good grades AND be a "cool" person? Why or why not?

_____

_____

_____

_____

_____

How did the artist handle the teasing that he went through?

_____

_____

_____

<u>Song 3. Dream Big</u>

Dreaming big

a) Can just lead to more frustration

b) Is only for "them" or "other" people

c) Can be done by anyone and can give purpose

Why do you think the song says that "Dreams are gonna take practice"?

_____

_____

_____

_____

_____

How much does it cost to Dream Big?

_____

_____

If you were going to Dream Big and create "the perfect life", what would that be like? Who is there? What are you doing and how does it feel to think about?

_____

_____

_____

_____

_____

_____

_____

_____

What does the following mean…?

"We all think of what is, instead of what *could* be".

_____

_____

_____

_____

_____

_____

Song 4. Beautiful

Which of the following most closely explains the message of the song?

   a) "Once they respect me, I will be okay"

   b) Respect yourself first and then they will respect you

   c) I have to be beautiful to gain respect

What is respect?

_____

_____

_____

_____

_____

_____

Is it more important to be beautiful on the inside or on the outside? Why do you think that?

_____

_____

_____

Out of everybody that you know, who respects you the most? And who do you respect the most? Why?

_____

_____

_____

_____

_____

Song 5. Focus

The Primary message of this song is…

a) If you focus on negative thoughts you will always be happy

b) The only options in life are to be rich or homeless

c) Good or bad, you will get what you focus on

If you continually think a thought over and over what does this song say will happen?

_____

_____

_____

What kind of thoughts do you think the President focused on as a kid?

_____

_____

_____

"**I am soooo cool**/What is wrong with me?/ **I hope I don't screw up!/** I am going to win" are some of the that lots of us think. What about you?

For the rest of the day, try to notice what thoughts enter your head most.

Song 6. False Idols

Are the artists saying that

a) You should believe everything rappers say in their songs

b) Sometimes rappers claim wrong doings because they think it will sell more records

c) It is important to analyze the lyrics we listen to every day

d) Both B & C

Who does the song say make the most money thanks to "gangsta rap" music?

_____

_____

_____

The song says that music is a lot like movies, why do they say that?

_____

_____

_____

_____

Have you ever looked up to somebody, who eventually turned out to be a "false idol"? If so, who?

_____

_____

_____

Song 7. Why Do you Wanna Fight?

Fighting someone during school hours can
a) Get you lots of respect
b) Get you suspended
c) Get you labeled a trouble maker by teachers
d) Both B & C
e) All of the above

Have you ever encountered a bully? Have you ever bullied someone? What was the result?

_____

_____

_____

Looking back, are you happy with the result of the situation? If not, what could have happened differently?

_____

_____

_____

_____

What does the song say about the way to handle a bully?

_____

_____

_____

_____

Song 8. Dan The Man

What was the evolution of Dan's Drug use?

_____

_____

_____

_____

Do you think what happened to Dan could ever happen to someone you know?

_____

_____

_____

_____

What happened to Dan's "party friends" in the end?

_____

_____

_____

Song 9. Within (The Mirror)

Do you think it is better to:

a) Keep some secrets from people (just in case)

b) Tell everyone everything about yourself

c) Don't tell anyone anything

Why?

_____

_____

_____

_____

Have you ever felt like someone sees things in you that you don't see? Or have you ever felt you are a different person on the inside than what others see on the outside? Please explain.

_____

_____

_____

_____

_____

Song 10. GUNS R US

What do you think about guns?

_____

_____

_____

_____

What would be the advantage in owning one? What would be the risk in owning one?

_____

_____

_____

_____

The artist says there is a difference between America and other countries when it comes to guns. What is the difference?

_____

_____

_____

_____

23. HOW TO BILL FOR HIP-HOP THERAPY

As you hopefully have gathered, Hip-Hop can heal. Hip-hop can inspire. Hip-hop can be a catalyst to meaningful therapy. In the "medical necessity" however there are a few important questions. The most important are often, "How does hip-hop relate to the diagnosis of a client?" and "Can we BILL for hip-hop rehabilitation sessions"?

Individual or group therapies and interventions are designed to:

a) Reduce mental disability and restore, improve or maintain functioning.

b) Be consistent with the goals of learning, development, independent living, and enhanced self-sufficiency.

Elligan (2007) stated that the particular way hip-hop is used in therapy should be consistent with the treatment goals of the client. A billable/fundable note has *strength based, measurable behaviors* which address the pathology of the client and link back to the client's diagnosis. Strength based perspectives can include: resiliency based goals, symptom reduction, increasing behaviors/capacities and coping/skill building goals.

It is important that your goal creations do not focus simply on symptom elimination; goals should give clients the opportunity to take responsibility in their own lives. The purpose in goals can be to create opportunity for options and to reinforce learning. In order to create a billable note, the following four goals should always be considered when creating a Rhymecology® intervention.

Diagnosis

Symptoms

Behavior

Techniques

Rhymecology® interventions can be specific exercises which address behavior caused by symptoms consistent with a client's diagnosis.

Many times your clients have violent tendencies and act out their suppressed rage on peers or family. Since hip-hop is can be a voice of anger and frustration, clients often feel it safer to use the rhyming prose to process their own anger or frustration than they would in a standard one on one session. The goal of the Rhymecology® module is to give clients a chance to express or act out the same anger by using rhyme/verse/written word. Example 1 is an example of how therapists can use Rhymecology® techniques to increase resiliency and address the *violent* symptoms in a client diagnosed with *oppositional defiant disorder.*

Hip-hop has been called the voice for the voiceless; it can be a great way to engage your clients who are withdrawn and present with isolative behavior. Example 2 is an example of how therapists can use a

Rhymecology® technique with a client diagnosed with *Dysthymia* and then write a billable note for the session.

Sometimes songs have a way of saying things that are difficult for your clients to verbalize themselves. The next chapter lists hip-hop songs which cover dozens of important topics from abortions to materialism to loss/grief to drugs. Example 3 is an example of how therapists can use songs (as in the next chapter) to help clients who have exchange *self medication* for self expression.

Just reading a verse out loud can shift a client's feelings in a moment. This is extremely important for clients who don't have positive self statements in their everyday vocabulary. Example 4 shows how one can use *visualization* to create prose which leads clients to see beyond their diagnosis or current prognosis.

These selected examples show the range of ways that one can bill by using hip-hop based exercises. These Rhymecology® techniques are created originally with hip-hop music in mind but can be also used in any musical genre in which lyrics are essential.

EXAMPLE 1

GOAL: Client will increase days free from violent outbursts from zero to one day per week.

BEHAVIOR: Client is diagnosed with oppositional defiant disorder. Client has a history of violent outbursts.. The client was showing a flat affect at the start of this session. Recently the client was suspended from school.

INTERVENTION: This MHS asked the client what had happened at school that caused him to lose his temper. This MHS made a list of the feelings that the client mentioned leading up to and after the incident. MHS then assisted the client in finding words that rhymed with his "feeling words". This MHS asked the client to use his rhyming words and phrases to re-create the incident which got him suspended. This MHS praised the client for sharing his feelings and also commented on the client's new tone of voice and body language during this exercise.

RESPONSE: The client was not able to explain what had happened at school that caused his suspension. The client was able to express feelings he had such as "anger" and "pissed off". The client was able to think of words that rhymed with his feelings which created a story about what he went through. As the client read his story that client shared that *"Yesterday some kids made me feel some anger/they called me a gangbanger/I thought it was a dis/and got really pissed"*. While reading his rhyme, the client appeared congruent and was then able to admit that whenever he feels "disrespected" he can only react with physical fight.

PLAN: Next session will be use the client's rhyme to understandi why being disrespected always leads to violence form the client.

EXAMPLE 2

<u>GOAL</u>: Client will increase minutes engaging with family or peers from one to three minutes per day.

<u>BEHAVIOR</u>: Client diagnosed as dysthymic. Client is withdrawn, isolative and states a feeling of hopelessness. Client has overbearing father and a history of being abused. Client has difficulty expressing himself. Recently the client has been becoming more isolative.

<u>INTERVENTION</u>: MHS began session by presenting hip-hop music to client correlated to clients own diagnosis. MHS used open ended questions which allowed client the freedom to process the feelings which that came up from listening to the music. When client could not come up with his own words, the MHS presented a paper with faces representing the possible feelings. They chose which words the faces symbolized then underneath wrote down words which rhymed them. This MHS asked the client to make a sentence using those words and then praised the client for using his voice in such manner.

<u>RESPONSE</u>: The client bobbed his head as he listened to the hip-hop CD and gradually was able to speak about which songs he liked and did not like. Client joined the therapist in picking symbols which he felt in his body when he listened to the music. The client could not create a song on this day but through the activity was able to express that his *"Dad makes him mad"*. The client then was able to admit there is one daily incident where his biological father verbally degrades him.

PLAN: Next session will be to create a role-play where the client creates lines in rhymes that represent what his father would say to him when angry.

EXAMPLE 3

GOAL: Client will increase the number of times he substitutes self expression for self medication from zero to two times per week.

BEHAVIOR: The client has history of smoking marijuana and drinking alcohol. Client has lived in seven foster homes in the past five years. Client shows flat affect. Client's mother passed away five years ago and client's father is in prison.

INTERVENTION: This MHS asked the client to write down one thing he loved, one thing he hated and a dream that he has. After hearing the clients answers, this MHS played the client a song called "Dear Mama", which is a hip-hop song about the artists love and appreciation for his biological mother. This MHS used open ended questions to see which emotions the client felt after hearing the lyrics of the song. This MHS gave the client a journal to use when he feels like he is missing his mother.

RESPONSE: The client shared that he "likes drinking" and "hates school" and dreams about "being with a family that loves me". The client stated that he missed his biological mother. The client was open to listening to the song. The client stated that he appreciated the line in the song where the artist said "*Even as a crack fiend mama, you always was a black queen mama*". Client shared that reminded him of "when Mom was doing drugs". This lead to the client sharing he "might have" started self medicating because he missed her and "because I was curious why she liked it".

PLAN: Client will create a song for his mother titled "Dear Mama", where he can tell her some of the things that he never got to say.

EXAMPLE 4.

GOAL: Client will increase positive self statements from zero to one per day.

BEHAVIOR: Client has a history of cutting. Client's mother is a drug abuser. The client has recently been moved out of her foster home. The client has been taken away from a life she was beginning to enjoy. The client's grades slipped and client has recently shown less confidence.

INTERVENTION: MHS asked about client dreams. MHS assisted the client in the making up words and rhymes which related to her dream of being an artist and an art teacher one day. MHS helped client visualize the feeling of joy she would attain by doing this and then led it back to her current reality by telling her that she needs to start focusing now. This MHS related her dream to his mental health goal by explaining that she needs to make good decisions, not lose her temper at pointless things, and succeed in academics in order to become an art teacher.

RESPONSE: The client shared that it was her dream to become an art teacher. When the client started coming up with rhyming words, she downplayed it by saying "But I can't rap". However the client was able to think of rhyming words and was honest with her mental health goal and her flat affect seemed to disappear for a short time. The client had lines such as *"I want to be an artist and make lots of money/ I will be real happy with my hubby calling me honey/ I will buy a house for my Mother/ It will feel so good to take care of my brothers"*. The client read the poem out loud and listened to the support counselor do it as well. The client shared that "it made me feel good" and "I feel excited because I can feel the dream come true when I read the poem".

PLAN: Next session will be to follow up with the client's home relationship with her grandmother and to see if the client is getting on track at school in regards to his goals.

24. S.O.D.A.S

To put it simply, things are easier remembered in rhyme. 99% of commercially successful songs have some sort of rhyme scheme. From childhood most of our memorable tunes are short rhymes. Your ABC's rhyme. Limericks do. Nursery rhymes do.

Rhymecology techniques incorporate rhyme whenever possible. Even (sometimes especially) short two line rhymes have a habit of sticking around in a child's mind. I often will leave a client with a line like "I wrote this cuz my hope is strong/good or bad you get what you focus on" or "Stay true to your heart/cuz its cool to be smart" and the like.

Over the years I have had my share of songs and poems on radio and television and each time there was a heavy focus on rhyme and meter. I often do them without music or a beat, as they often take away from the message being sent.

The following poem is an example of using rhyme and meter to explain" Social Problem Solving and Decision-Making Techniques for working with Transitional Age Youth and Young Adults". (An Evidence Supported Technique created by Hewitt B. Clark). It is recommended for use with clients who are in TAY and/or TIP and make questionable decisions.

The first thing you do

When you're placed in a difficult *S*ituation
Is assess exactly, what it is that you're facing

It's important to name the problems

Before you'll be able to solve them
Once you know that

'
Then it's time to focus

On all the *O*ptions and possible approaches
Just think about solving the problem in whole
And what you can do to achieve your goal
But before you get locked in
Look closely at each and every option

"What's the *d*isadvantage to this?

And *a*dvantage the to that?"
Because it's always better to act
When you know the situation, options and facts.
You've now gone through the process and evolution

Of creating a successful *S*olution!

25. HELPFUL HIP-HOP

When most people think of hip-hop music a particular image comes into their minds. Unfortunately, more often than not, the images are sexual and violent. There is much more to the music than that! Even within hip-hop there are many genres towards which a fan can gravitate towards. Types of hip-hop and some of their artists include:

East Coast- Run Dmc, Eric B & Rakim (personal favorite), Nas, Wu-Tang Clan

West Coast- Kendrick Lamar, The Game, N.W.A., Jurassic 5

Southern- Outkast, Lil Wayne, Rick Ross, T.I

Christian Rap- tobyMac, Lecrae, BB Jay, Trip Lee

Country Rap- Bubba Sparxxx, Colt Ford, Cowboy Ford, Nappy Roots

Nerdcore- MC Frontalot, MC Hawking, YT Kracker, Optimus Rhyme

Jazz Rap- Guru, Jazzmatazz (album)

Trip Hop/Alternative- Antimatter, Zion 1, Gotye, Dub Pistols

Super Lyrical- Eminem, AZ, Royce da 5'9", Elzhi

Indie Hip-Hop- Little Brother, Sage Francis, Atmosphere, Immortal Technique

Old School- Afrika Bambaattaa, DJ Kool Herc, Grandmaster Flash, Treacherous Three

*Golden Age (1987-*1993)- Gangstarr, Big Daddy Kane, De La Soul, Public Enemy

Conscious- Talib Kweli, Common, A Tribe Called Quest, Mos Def (recommend all)

Commercial Rap- 50 Cent, Will Smith…well it's all commercially viable now.

Commercial rap is what one can hear on the radio and television every day. Commercial rap has become filled with so called ex-drug dealers boasting about champagne filled bath tubs, designer clothes and cars and the importance of wearing diamonds most of its listeners can't afford. Somewhere along the way it was decided that music with these kinds of messages should be promoted, instead of all other types.

While we cannot change the industry and what the media decides is worthy to promote to our kids, what we can do is give our kids options. In this section I will lay out hip hop songs which deal with real life issues in educational and inspirational ways. However, not only are they thought provoking, the listed songs are *good songs, by good artists.*

They are classic hip-hop songs that range from the year 1988 to 2008. There will be a few explicit lyrics here and there, but they will be few and far between. When they are used, the curse is used to accentuate the point or in the creative context.

If your clients really enjoy hip-hop, they will enjoy these songs. If your client listens to hip-hop and these songs don't have any impact on the client, I would suggest that he/she has already been seduced by the hip-hop formula of sex, money and violence. The following is hope.

The Rhymecology® Message Mix

-The Message of the song

-The Title of the song (in "quotes")

-The Artist (directly following the song title)

-Lines from one of the selected songs

Respect For Women

1)"**U.N.I.T.Y**"- Queen Latifah

2)**" Faithful"-** Common

"Instinct leads me to another flow

Everytime I hear a brother call a girl a bitch or a ho

Trying to make a sister feel low

You know all of that gots to go… "

- Queen Latifah

Materialism

"**Loves Gonna Get'cha**"- Boogie Down Productions

2) "**All Falls Down**"- Kanye West

"So, for future reference remember it's alright to like or want a material Item, but when you fall in love with it and you start scheming and carrying on for it, just remember, it's gonna get'cha… "

- Boogie Down Productions

Loss Grief

1) **"One More Dance"** - Nas

2) **"You Never Know"** - Immortal Technique

"I wish you were here,

I miss you more each second I breathe

You resting in peace forever I accepted you free… "

- Nas

Mom Songs

1) **"Dear Mama"** - Tupac

2) **"U Let Me Grow"** - eMC

"I finally understand

for a woman it ain't easy tryin to raise a man

You always was committed

A poor single mother on welfare, tell me how ya did it

There's no way I can pay you back

But the plan is to show you that I understand… "

-Tupac

Politics

1) **"New World Water"** - Mos Def

2) **"Fight The Power"** - Public Enemy

"There are places where TB is common as TV

Cause foreign-based companies go and get greedy

The type of cats who pollute the whole shore line

Have it purified, sell it for a dollar twenty-five…" -Mos Def

<u>Drugs</u>

1)"**Dan The Man**"- J.Walker & Gilli Moon

2) "**Get By**"- Talib Kweli

"This morning, I woke up

Feeling brand new and I jumped up

Feeling my highs, and my lows

In my soul, and my goals

Just to stop smokin, and stop drinkin

And I've been thinkin - I've got my reasons…"

-Talib Kweli

<u>Sex & Aids</u>

1)"**Aids is Gold H.I.V is Platinum**"- Canibus

2) "**Let's Talk About Sex**"- Salt N Pepa

" …most people don't question

the person they having sex with

as to whether or not they infected

Even the people you already slept wit

wouldn't suspect that they can catch it

Forty percent of the AIDS patients is Afro-Americans

And we only twelve percent of the population

That statement is a fact, latinos and blacks face it

It came straight from the World Health Organization…"

-Canibus

Pregnancy & Abortion

1)**"Brendas Got A Baby"**- Tupac

2) **"Retrospect for Life"**- Common

> "There's too many black women that can say they mothers
>
> but can't say that they wives
>
> I wouldn't chose any other to mother my understanding
>
> But I want our Parenthood to come from Planning
>
> It's so much in my life that's undone
>
> We gotta see eye to eye, about family, before we can become one… "
>
> -Common

Gangs

1)**"We're All in the Same Gang"**- West Coast All Stars

2) **"Self Destruction"**- Stop The Violence Movement

> "Brothers killin other brothers
>
> I thought the idea was to love one another?
>
> Open up the paper to one more death
>
> If y'all keep this up then there'll be no one left… "
>
> - West Coast All Stars

Inspirational

1)**"I Can"**- Nas

2) **"I Will Make It"**- KRS-One

"Be, B-Boys and girls, listen up

You can be anything in the world, in God we trust

An architect, doctor, maybe an actress

But nothing comes easy it takes much practice… "

- Nas

Education

1)"**Why Is That**"-Boogie Down Productions

2) "**You Must Learn**"- Boogie Down Productions

"The age of the ignorant rapper is done

Knowledge Reigns Supreme Over Nearly Everyone

The stereotype must be lost

That love and peace and knowledge is soft…"

-Boogie Down Production

26. THE (W)RAP UP

We've come to the end of the guide and the beginning of your healing through hip-hop music and culture. If you purchased this guide, chances are that you already had an inkling about the healing properties that writing, journaling, music and art can bring. Hip-hop encapsulates all of those.

These techniques will not work with every client. These techniques will not work with every therapist. One day Rhymecology may work, one day it may not. But when working with urban adolescents, I hope you have Rhymecology as an option.

When you are working on a house, one day you may need your hammer. Another day, the screwdriver. The next day you might need the wrench. All of these tools are imperative to your handiwork but they are not all necessary at the same time. All of these Rhymecology techniques add up to one tool in your therapy belt. When you have that option to reach for that tool, you are building a bridge for youth to walk across. When they can feel safe walking across that bridge they open themselves up to healing.

Thank you for all that you do. Your make a difference and that is the best thing in the world.

ABOUT THE AUTHOR

Jeffrey T. Walker, M.A. is a Qualified Mental Health Professional who has worked with youth at-risk for 15 years. He has focused his work in the high risk areas of Long Beach, Compton and South Los Angeles. The "Rhymecologist" brings the science of psychology and his passion for music together to help people feel empowered, and to feel better about themselves and the world they live in. He uses hip hop culture and lyrics as therapeutic/educational tools through motivational programs, media, workshops, music and literature.

Over the years he has had writing and music featured on/in 60 Minutes, TNT's Inside the NBA, at the Staples Center, the Oakland Coliseum, and was the Resident Poet on Fox Sports Radio for 10 years. He has won numerous Poetry Slams and performed/taught in places such as British Columbia, Bermuda, Australia, Fiji, Denmark, Paris and Rome.

See more of Jeff Walker on his websites www.rhymecology.com (the mission) and www.jwalkerthepoet.com (the man).

RHYMECOLOGY® PRODUCTS

SKillz CD: A therapeutic tool for teenagers!

www.skillzCD.com

The author of this guide is available for workshops, presentations and performances for your company or organization. Topics include;

- "Healing youth with Hip-Hop" (For Therapists)
- "Skillz for Life" (Interactive performance for youth)
- "Rhymecology® writing workshops" (Group song writing)
- "Song Camp" (Youth writing and performance)

References

Alvarez, T. (2011). "Beats, Rhymes and Life": Rap Therapy in an Urban Setting. In S. Hadley & G. Yancy (Eds.), *Therapeutic Uses of Rap and Hip-Hop* (pp. 337-352). New York: Taylor & Francis Group.

Bostic, J., Pataki, C., Rho, Y., Schlozman, S., & Martin, A. (2006). Rebels without a cause? Adolescents and their anti-heroes. *Psychiatric Times, 23*(10), 26.

Coholic, D. (2011). Exploring the feasibility and benefits of arts-based mindfulness-based practices with young people in need: Aiming to improve aspects of self-awareness and resilience. *Child & Youth Care Forum, 40*(4), 303-317. doi:10.1007/s10566-010-9139-x

Chong, H. & Kim, S. (2010). Education-oriented music therapy as an after-school program for students with emotional and behavior problems. *The Arts in Psychotherapy, 37*(3), 190-196. doi:10.1016/j.aip.2010.03.004

Edgar, K. (1979). A case of poetry therapy. *Psychotherapy, 16*(1), 104-106. doi:10.1037/hoo85863

Elligan, D. (2007). Rap therapy: A culturally sensitive approach to psychotherapy with young African American men. *Journal of African American Studies, 5*(3), 1936-4741. doi: 10.1007/s12111-000-1002-y

Faulker, S. (2011). Drumbeat: In search of belonging. *Youth Studies Australia, 30*(2), 9-14.

Haaken, J., Wallin-Ruschman, J., & Pantage, S. (2012). Global hip-hop identities: Black youth, psychoanalytic action research, and the moving to the beat project. *Journal of Community & Applied Social Psychology, 22*(1), 63-74. doi:10.1002/casp.1097

Jocson, K. (2006). "Bob Dylan and Hip Hop": Intersecting literacy practices in youth poetry communities. *Written Communication. 23* (3), 231. doi:10.1177/0741088306288154

Kobin, C., & Tyson, E. (2006). Thematic analysis of Hip-Hop music: Can Hip-Hop in therapy facilitate empathic connections when working with clients in urban settings? *The Arts in Psychotherapy, 33*(4), 343-356. doi:10.1016/j.aip.2006.05.001

Mahiri, J. (2006). Digital DJ-ing: Rhythms of learning in an urban school. *Language Arts, 84*(1), 55-62.

McFerran, K. (2011). Music therapy with bereaved youth: Expressing grief and feeling better *Prevention Researcher, 18*(3), 17-20.

McFerran, K., Roberts, M., & O'Grady, L. (2020). Music therapy with bereaved teenagers: A mixed methods perspective. *Death Studies, 34*(6), 541-565. doi:10.1080/07481181003765428

Morrell, E., & Ducan-Andrade, J. (2002). Promoting academic literacy with urban youth through engaging hip-hop culture. *English Journal, 91*(6), 88.

O'Brien, E. (2011). "Morphine Mamma": Creating Original Songs Using Rap with Women with Cancer. In S. Hadley & G. Yancy (Eds.), *Therapeutic Uses of Rap and Hip-Hop* (pp. 337-352). New York: Taylor & Francis Group.

Petersson, G., & Nystrom, M. (2011). Music: Artistic performance or a therapeutic tool? A study on differences. *International Journal of Music Education, 29*(3), 229-240. doi:10.1177/0255761411408498

Selfout, M., Delsing, M., Boft, T., & Meeus, W. (2008). Heavy metal and Hip-Hop style preferences and externalizing problem behavior. A two-wave longitudinal study. *Youth and Society, 39*(4), 435-452.

Spillane-Grieco, E. (2004). From parent verbal abuse to teenage physical aggression? *Child and Adolescent Social Work Journal, 17*(6), 1573-2797. doi:10.1023/A:1026427710320

Stephens, D. (2007). The effects of images of African American women in hip hop on early adolescents' attitudes toward physical attractiveness and interpersonal relationships. *Sex Roles, 56*(3-4), 1573-2762. doi:10.1007/s11199-006-9145-5

Stephens, T., Braithwaite, R., & Taylor, S. (1998). Model for using hip-hop music for small group HIV/AIDS prevention counseling with African American adolescents and young adults. *Patient Education and Counseling, 35*(2). 127-137. doi:10.1016/S07383991(98)00050-0

Turner-Musa, J., Rhodes, W., Harper, P., & Quinton, S. (2008). Hip-Hop to prevent substance use and HIV among African-American youth: A preliminary investigation. *Journal of Drug Education, 38* (4), 351-365. doi:10.2190/DE.384.c

Tyson, E. H. (2002). Hip Hop therapy: An exploratory study of a rap music intervention with at-risk and delinquent youth. *Journal of Poetry Therapy, 15*(4), 131-144. Washington, D., Beecher, D. (2010).

Music as social medicine: Two perspectives on the West-Eastern divan orchestra. *New Directions for Youth Development)*, 127-140.

RHYMECOLOGY

The Rhymecologist can be reached at:

rhymecology@gmail.com

www.rhymecology.com

www.facebook.com/rhymecology

References

www.ingramcontent.com/pod-product-compliance
Lightning Source LLC
Chambersburg PA
CBHW081218280526
45787CB00006B/2435